TULE REVIEW
WINTER 2011

SPC
SACRAMENTO
POETRY CENTER

TULE REVIEW
WINTER 2011

Editors
Theresa McCourt and Linda Collins

Layout
Susan Davis Hyman

Cover Design
Richard Hansen

Cover Artist
Thomas Leaver

Special Thanks to the Following
The Albert and Elaine Borchard Foundation
The Estate of Anatole Lubovich
Mimi and Burnett Miller
Friends of Quinton Duval
Sacramento Metropolitan Arts Commission

Sacramento
Metropolitan
Arts Commission

Published by Sacramento Poetry Center Press
Sacramento Poetry Center
1719 25th Street
Sacramento, CA 95816
Ph: 916-979-9706
www.sacramentopoetrycenter.org

Please see our submission guidelines for the next Tule Review
http://sacpoetrycenter.wordpress.com/tule-review/

SACRAMENTO
POETRY CENTER

Published by
Sacramento Poetry Center,
a not-for-profit,
tax-exempt organization
registered in the state of
California. Contributions
to the review and the
organization are welcome
and tax-deductible.

ISBN-10 0983136203
ISBN-13 9780983136200

Cover Artist Details
Artist: Thomas Leaver
Material: Oil on panel
Size: 64 to 54 inches
Title: "Tacit"

Contents

Joyce Odam

A Town of Old Hotels

When I traveled to the town of Sorrow,
bringing my old suitcase

full of stones,
and I was long in arriving

where it was cold,
where it was raining,

where doors hung blindly
waiting for me to choose one

but the town was full of doors,
no knobs, no numbers,

a town of old hotels where all my
old loves were waiting,

dreamed, and lying shadowless
and strange.

Had they forgotten me?
Was I soon enough to hold them?

Timothy Sandefur

Escaping

I tripped into Missouri, parched
With common dust. Not looking for nothing,
Not even for freedom. That I had
Already. Had Jesus' love and my daughters;
My fate, broken in; and the river at dawn,
When blackbirds dart and skip across
The water. I didn't have no mission,
Or want to stand for someone's proof;
Was proof enough for Harriet
Without a world to know my name.
I knew the boundaries, if nothing else.

But the river in the morning sun
Reflects its light on both of us,
You on your side, me on mine,
And its judging heat makes our eyes all swell
And tear alike, whatever they say.
Over there was the future rising
Rising up, rising north,
Rising like that morning sun,
And - no matter what they say tonight -
Yes, I think I'm rising too.
At dawn, I'm gonna wash away this dust.

JoAnn M. Anglin

Late Morning

Sometimes I look out my west-facing
window, see the shadow of my roof
and on that shadow roofline, birds
walking. When the shadow birds take
flight, I wonder. How I trust those
silhouettes, their lift and grace, clean, silky
shapes rippling across the grass. Things
inside my house have surfaces, edges,
make sounds if I hit them: Bang! Click!
Ding! Yet how they perplex me,
unlike the shadow roof of shadow birds.

Dennis Hock

Mockingbird

Each morning I waken
to a mockingbird's plagiarized notes
breaking over my window sill.

Why do I like his audacity?

All day, I move through a range
of my own imitations
pretending each is an actual me.

See how complex
and varied
and multitudinous
I am, I warble.

Yet I don't feel audacious at all.

Where's he get his self-assurance
that little thief?
By what dispensation his right
to be a singular and bold fraud?

Another question nags me:
can we ever become what we steal?

To stopper his shameless impersonating
I try closing my window at night
but then he awakens in my head,
at precisely 5 a.m., to remind me
another day awaits more petty forgery.

How easily
I submit.

I open my mouth,
then my throat.

Geoff Stevens

Submaximal Responses

Sleep is my diving suit
takes me down
below the illuminated walls of my retina memories
to where fearsome creatures roam
with their phosphorescent head probes
and albino eyes
to seek answers to the unfathomable.
But if I tug on the line
while images are clear
nobody winds me up
and findings flounder
in that ocean space of time that nitrogen has
to flood my blood with bends and other intricacies of shape
meanderings of reality
so when I reach the shore of day
they come mumbo-jumbo out
destroy the truth
its depth charge revelations night rated
explosions held back until next shift.

Marie Reynolds

Girl, Asylum, Chevrolet

The nurse rolls a steel cart down
the hall. Take these, she says, and shoves
a paper cup at me. Three white pills.
It's not pills I need, but someone
to turn off the overhead lights and this
incessant gibberish, a cool hand
on my flushed skin, someone to drive

the car inside me - a two-tone Chevy
like the one Daddy owned - with its plush
back seat, big enough for me to stretch
out on. Just let me rest. I'll know that I'm home
though my eyes are closed, by the way
the car slows and starts up the grade, by the sound
of tires on the crushed gravel drive.

Frank Praeger

Some Distance, Some Flowers

The distant in the slow and elegiac,
autumn -
the turning, arcing of yellowing tasseled grass.
Blue lost in a still further blue,
dense patches of white mallow.
Purple thistle, blue chicory at morning's outer edge.
Kids playing.
Two crows calling
as I continue walking,
aged,
     with a finality to every present thought,
yet, happy -
        happy as I've ever been?

I cannot say.

I had not been so aware of the succession of days.

Changming Yuan

Poppies: Parallel Poem

Each pair of round lips
Cut right in the middle
Bleeding so boldly
In foggy fields
Of a forgotten season

Nobody to kiss
Nobody to talk with
All like blood-skirted pasts
Painted thickly
Close to the heart

Lyn Lifshin

The Horses at Night

The moon, a plate.
Too heavy, half
sinking into the
mist. Silver leaves,
the faintest stars.
Milkweed and
tumbleweed.
Before black ice,
the still Vermont
roads, a cocoon,
wraps us past
willows and farm
houses and there,
in a field, the
horses half blend
into each other,
close as girls at
recess. Beautiful,
unsure in my car
lights, caught like
stars in a paparazzi
glare. I don't want
to leave, stunned
until suddenly, as
if on cue, it begins
to thunder and hail.
Then the horses
turn silver.

Joanne Lowery

Angel as Spectator

It took most of heaven's morning
for wings to poke and fluff themselves,
for me to learn to balance a halo.

By noon in that supreme brightness
I could see everything below: the seventeen wars
currently in progress, their journalistic details.

Here and there someone reading, a child
on a swing, a car missing a stop sign,
a team of geologists measuring a crack.

My eyes were busy but I had no brain
to remember the panorama. Nothing made sense,
not even the tracks through the Midwest

made yesterday by someone like me.
Snow had begun to cover them
with small round feathers.

The space they traveled through
was perfectly empty: wingless and windless
where nothing divine happens.

Robert Childers

Catching Songs

Chief Marie,
Cordova's last speaker
of the Eyak language,
saw her final days coming,
requested a gathering
at the old village site
abandoned for years,
now returned to the forest.

At the drum,
two singers hummed
a song neither
had heard before.
They queried their elder,
who explained in patient manner
the obvious.

"Look around you," she said.
"These mountains, these trees,
they remember those songs
our people once sung here,
and return them
to those who will listen."

Richard Luftig

Obbligato for Bass Fiddle

Restless
staccato
reducing
the art
of drumming
to brush strokes
mezzo piano
to single
chords

Cool
bottom
voice
lowering
the pulse
of the room
to single
beats
resting
at
the precipice
between
fingers
and string

Unmeasured
cloistered
shutting down
shutting up
every
other
instrument
keeping
even
Gabriel's
trumpet
waiting

Philip Dacey

For Clara Lee, at Juilliard

Barefoot cellists wash their feet
beforehand
in a long pour of notes.

The Bach unaccompanied suites
accompanied by
the curling and uncurling
of toes.

Feet mostly flat
on the stage floor
to pick up signals
from below.

Not afraid
of splinters
in the music.

The eyes of so many listeners
stealing down to sight-read
a pair of feet.

Bach never
before so
naked.

Afterwards, the feet
left unwashed for days
to retain the scent of sound.

Philip Dacey

In Praise of Certain Slow Movements
at Juilliard

The notes move on the air
the way a hand
follows the contours
of a naked body.

An almost-silence
in which to hear
another silence.

One note follows another because
the previous has taken the time
to think the next
carefully
into existence.

The rhythm here
feels familiar.
Ah - the amniotic fluid.

If this movement were only
a little slower,
time and its effects
would be erased.

I can't tell if
at this speed we,
blessedly, arrive
at a human core or,
equally blessedly,
leave the human behind.

Marie Reynolds

Primer

1.

Sometimes – without warning – the narrow gate
opens and we pass through it. When we try
to find the gate again it is gone.
What we can't comprehend makes us human.

2.

A woman walks to the river alone, tule fog
deepening. Birds in flight call to her.
She follows the sound. To believe
in what we cannot see - this, too, is simply human.

3.

In autumn the man in the wheelchair
pauses beneath a gingko tree. Each day he loses
a little more strength. Yellow light, yielding leaf -
what it means to be human.

James Valvis

For Yourself

Save a little love
for yourself. The rest
give away. Give it
to your friend trying
to forget life,
the dog that barks at you
when you walk,
the woman who doesn't call.
Give it to your mother
and to God, if you care to.
Give it away, mostly,
but save a little for yourself.
You'll need it.
Keep a little by you, always.
Hide some around the house
like a bottle of scotch,
like a pipe when
lonely, or maybe set it up
like a mistress, in another town,
waiting, a kept emotion.
No matter what anyone says,
what is promised,
save some love for yourself.
Save a little
it will come in handy.

John Grey

Woman in Her Garden

I married you
for your ripe red tomatoes,
those fat green cukes,
and the beets and carrots,
pulled from the earth,
with the best earth
still inside them.

I said to myself
she grows beans . . .
love that.
She plants potatoes.
Direct your affection
in just such a cause.
And what about
the kale and the onion?
Passion by another name.

Lie down in her bed,
I told myself.
Be furrowed
seeded
watered
fertilized.
Be picked
placed before me
at my very own table.

I married you
for how good I'd taste.

Briony Gylgayton

In Parts Only

Each thrust like gulping champagne,
seeing the parts slide
and steam struggling between,
his sweat reminds me
of rain on rocks and how in dakota
there are basins no one has touched,
only by rat noses
dampening the edges.

I would go deep into them,
fast, so my body goes flat
in the canyon bed,
and crows could sweep over me,
if they liked,
gather on my body,
until my hips shock them
into the air again.
Like the crows, so many of my favorite things are in parts
and I've seen many bodies in parts only.

Changming Yuan

Internal Dryness

According to traditional Chinese medicine,
some conditions result from internal dryness.

In this lower mainland, rain is the order
Of the day: the drizzle moisturizes
Dreams and drama alike, storms have filled
Every crack and crevice with seasonal juice

But deep in your body has been a drought
Persisting ever since your birth, no plant
Grows green enough, no bird comes to perch
On a bough, all pipes and rivulets dry

Oh, for a rich rain to moisten and irrigate your
Inner fields, your cells, your nerves, your hopes
I would sacrifice my fatherhood, provided you
Could take a shower in the open, with your spine
Stemming straight like a strong young tree

Anna Erickson

Clean Shaven, Violent Vocal Cords

My sweet friend
He walks the streets with an honesty
despair doesn't know.
He dines on sandpaper,
Voice rasping with blood.

Because his organs are bruised
Hung like horror movie props
Up and down his arms.
And he knows when I am holding my drink
With two hands.

He told me
Love is like a scale that never finds balance.
And that you can smile your way through a sea of beauty
And never let it reach your eyes.

Because he seems to see in different shades of blue.
He has hands made of bristles and
I like it when he talks about plant genuses.
His hoarse laugh erupts in muted tones.
It makes my stomach less empty.

And because he knows sorrow and joy
are all just the same thing.

Alan Catlin

A Moveable Calvary in Central Florida

The self-proclaimed penitent
of Central Florida drags his
homemade cross down soft
shoulders, marking his time
of great suffering in dust &
disturbed stone, carrying his
burden from one flea market
tent to the next as if all this
carrying will somehow lighten
the loads of fellow travelers,
bargain shoppers, haunters
of defunct strip malls converted
into places of worship, white
elephant tag sales & he the
emissary that must bridge both
worlds, the sacred & the profane,
plastic grapes attached to his
imitation crowd of thorns, rubbing
his forehead raw, filthy robes
made from fitted sheets, sandaled
feet real rubber soles cobbled
together from car tires and beach
thongs, all part of the image he
must project, the message he is
trying to convey: a discount jesus
is dying for your sins.

David Dickson

On Being Alone With the World

I haven't often felt the presence
calling from the distant Spirit World.
And yet it can happen. Even after
too many years in the work world and
the burdens of a busy, family life.
It can still happen. Like that cool Fall night
when I stepped from my car into small town
life and began walking up Main Street toward
the Mill Pond when a light wind moved past me,
so gently, it made me stop and grin.
Another sweet moment that I took with me
all the way to my seat in the café
where I ordered coffee and tried to read
from a book of poems I could not understand.
At least not then, with the three women
at the next table distracting me
with their stories of infertility,
long work hours and difficult men. Stressful,
detailed stories that somehow started to lift
their voices, like atavistic spirits
rising to restore their faith, until they
were laughing and planning, and I was
smiling all the way back into the night.
Where the wind had picked up and turned colder.

Gene McCormick

The Restaurant Business: 2010

Not busy at The Greek's tonight.
Two old male waiters lock arms
do a few slow dance turns
near the bar to a mazurka,
quietly sing homeland lyrics.

Later they compare tip notes.
A table of three left Tony a 67c tip;
Spend it wisely, says bald Alex,
patting his pocket.
Crazy Shirley left me 10c.

Dancing, music, singing, money.
Less can be more.

Clint Margrave

Bar'd

I walked into a poem the other night.

It had been a long day
and I happened to see a
sign with a great big beckoning
arrow calling me.

Just one, I promised myself.

A couple other guys
I recognized were standing in front,
chain smoking,
pacing back and forth,
deciding whether to go in.

I didn't hesitate.

I walked straight up to the entrance
where a white bearded bouncer
met me and asked if I had
any identification.

He looked at it for a while
and I thought for sure
he was going to deny me.

"It's slow tonight kid," he said finally,
handing it back, "don't expect to get lucky."

I thanked him
and went in anyway.

He was right.
No music played,
no flames were alight,
the muses had all been thrown out.

It was not my kind of poem.

Marilyn Wallner

Mirabile Dictu
for Richard Jones

I have discovered a new poet.
More auspicious than discovering
a continent.
And what would I at my age
do with a continent?
A poet's of far greater value.
He (for this is a man) tells me
of his frailties, tells me
how I can set my moral compass
to produce less self-judgmental readings.
Brings forth the tears that come
with recognition
of a fellow pilgrim
on the road to Damascus.
He exhorts me to write poetry
because "a poem left unwritten dies and
you become a walking tomb, a whitewashed sepulcher."
I know where he teaches
but I won't stalk him, rather
I will buy his books,
keep them close for
therein lies his voice.

Clint Margrave

The First Time Books Saved My Life

You know why kids don't value books these days?
Because they've never been smacked
with my mother's wooden spoon.
She threatened me with it whenever I acted up.

This one time, I really outsmarted her.

I went into my room,
pulled two thin hard covers off my bookshelf,
and stuffed them in the back of my underpants,
just as she was coming after me.

When the spoon finally struck, the books padding my ass
snapped the wood in two pieces,
hurling splinters across the entryway,
shocking us both.

This was the first time books saved my life.

And I learned to value them like a monk
learns to value solitude -
even if they didn't do shit when her hand
slammed across my face shortly afterward.

Brad Henderson

beige townhouse
orange county, ca

lollygagging in bed
once again. it is the 80s
the sheets are mauve & satin
my mullet is bent & smashed
were i still to have a job
i would've been hours
at a desk, yet it is 11 am
& i am prone, sipping coffee
sticky from punkish dreams
of trade paperbacks to rival
McInerney & Janowitz

fuck the poet, cowboy, athlete,
& drummer—better to drink like a
best-selling novelist. blocks away
the 405 freeway rumbles
5-by-5-lane channels of hunkish
jism—what once i knew as
bull blood supreme. so much
anxious motion & decimated
depth & breadth down here in
greater Los Angeles—maybe later
i will call my grandmother
whom i still talk w/ every week
& ask her if this new egg smell
of sunshine & dew
means i will never make it back
to Oak Meadows Ranch

JoAnn M. Anglin

Homemaking

we girls made homes of leaves
with autumn's sycamore bounty
wafting from branches arced
across school grasses
we scooped and spread rectangle
rooms, brown and yellow
and this is the front door, we'd say
a bedroom, kitchen, garage
the bathroom left out, early
learning what not to speak of
you be the father
you the sister
you be the baby - wah, wah
during lunchtime, constructing our
futures with leaves already crumbling
walls would be walked over, floor plans
kicked through, decayed in first rains
our visions blown away with the
first pushing winds.

Gaylord Brewer

3305 Linnet for Sale

As I sketch the rooms' contours
all seems in place, though dimensions distend.
A great opening between living room -
free-swinging gold-gilt lamps and Mannequin Piss
fountain (hi-brow vs. low, my folks were funny) -
and "wreck" room where living happened.
Bay windows over groping wisteria,

leather couch, rabbit-eared TV, Nixon resigning
perhaps my earliest historical memory
pinpointed (leaving aside Apollo 17,
Tracy's panties that afternoon in the garage).
This drawing claims a space, cognizant
of failure (talent, mind) or a thing yet to emerge.
The square of a white house, on the street

of the sweet, fleeting linnet, will not close.
My mother in the kitchen somewhere,
or on the screened porch with the bald cardinal
her seasonal pet. Or, I mean to say, mailing
a real estate clipping to her son thirty years on,
a post-it we should all have just stayed
and we'd have made out as well, maybe better.

Fred Longworth

My Friend James Has Died

and in memoriam, his two sons and daughter
have moved a dumpster into the backyard
and filled it with forty-five years
of his anthropological research.

Eleven bookcases stand vacant, and I see
his rosewood desk in an antique shop
on 19th Street, priced at $2995.
The 14th-century shaman's mask from Borneo
has made the journey to Sotheby's website.

The older son informs me that the Persian carpets
are worthless because of foot-traffic and bugs.
No one seems to know what's happened
to the dark green 1958 Jaguar.

I admire the new Rolex on the younger son's wrist,
and wish I could hand-letter as well as
the daughter. A big sign over the front door reads:
ESTATE SALE - 8 TO 5 - SAT AND SUN -
EVERYTHING MUST GO.

Penelope Vaillancourt

The Closing of the Mouth Ceremony 2

A long wooden staff in his right hand
Blue strips of cloth draped his face, his body
And when he came in the room
His feet did not touch the floor
A cold breeze
Like someone blowing in your ear and
A scent of roses filled the room
I asked, do you smell that?
No one noticed.
I told my three sisters
Death just passed by
My sister cautioned me with fear,
Don't say that, but it was too late.
I already knew
I looked at my father pale and
Struggling to breathe
His face turning to wax.

One time long, long ago
We were traveling along an old dirt road
In the hot and bone dry woods of Northern California
Sun shining in the heat of a summer day
Dusty rooster tails following
The old green Ford truck down the road
A golden eagle sat on top of a burned telephone.
My dad slowed down and pulled over
We all got out, and he reached
Behind the seat for his rifle
He was a sharpshooter and would never miss
I looked at him, the bird, the rifle
And yelled - Go bird, go!
Ping! The bullet hit the pole
And left a trail of white smoke
The eagle flew off into the trees for cover.
My dad yelled and slapped me across the face
He told me to get in the back of the truck

I wanted him to
Hold me in his lap so
I could rest my head on his chest
And listen to his heart beat.

On the bed wrapped in white sheets
One tear fell from his left eye,
He raised his arms
And cried out, "Oh, my God."

At that moment, I believed in God
Seeing with my own eyes
Dying and Death itself
Passing me by like that and
I wondered why he let me see him
Come into the room.

My sisters ran out screaming.
I stayed behind
For The Closing of the Mouth Ceremony
Begging,
Nurse, Please help me fix his yawning mouth
What does it matter, she asked, aren't you cremating him?
It's for them I said pointing to the closed door.
For them
It took two of us -
Like shutting a door in the wind
To shove his jaw shut
I closed his eyes -
If I had two gold coins I would have
Placed them properly on his eyelids
To pay for his passage across the river.

Heather Altfeld

Snow in April
after a line by Raymond Carver

If things stood as they had before,
I would be spending my morning
climbing through the tangle of the garage
to find the small wooden breakfast tray
for the tiny vase of flowers,
the Broadway bagel - sesame, scrambled egg
and cheese. If I would just turn the radio up
and the children down,
climb into bed beside him,
rest my leg against his,
listen to Scott Simon's
these are a few voices from the news...
while we ate.

If things stood as they had before
and his computer screen gleamed low
late into the night,
and the children, enraptured with
scissors or nude bathing in the wading pool
nubbed only fisted waves of their busy little hands
at his homecoming.
Then, he could once again step into the kitchen
where I was preparing the next meal,
step in at my dogged requests for
drinks, napkins, forks - some attempt
at help or hope. If things stood
as they had before, we would eat
with our minds on what came next - baths, stories,
that computer terminal, making love
while a video played in the other room,
bolting up afterward to lead the routine.

And if things stood as they had before,
I would spend nights looking out the window
for some kind of rescue, or clue,

some word from the universe, some direction,
or even - just a little starlight, the graze of the moon
against the blinds - if they stood as they had before
I would still be dreaming and he still asleep,
I wondering if there was some way
I could count to the end,
like hide and seek or kick the can,
some way I could know that love was beyond comfort,
that it demands more than the simple request
for water at the bedside,
or please, close the window
for sake of chill.
If things stood as they had before,
I would understand longing
like a Northeasterner come mid-April
who wakes to ice crystals on the window,
slant of snow in the drive,
and calls down the stairs
to no one in particular,
when will spring come?
When will the fucking spring come?

Marie Reynolds

The Fisherman's Wake

It's raining again. At the Salty Quill
I order a pint of whatever's on tap. My black
skirt's tight, black stockings snagged.
I close my eyes. The little life we stitched
together stares back at me like a blind
fish eye. I practice saying the word
out loud: widow . . . widow . . . almost . . .
window. Window . . . an opening
through which light can enter.
Everything seems to hinge on this.
I drain my glass. The room spins.
Someone puts another drink
in my hand. All these bodies press
together - cattle in a pen - river of steam,
sweat, yeasty breath, wet flesh, rough
shoulders, ruddy ears. Roars of laughter.
I whisper his name. I'm all alone. I'm not
alone. There's a hand on my hand, a mouth
on my mouth. I'm wearing a felt,
wide-brimmed hat, fine black netting
over my eyes. Someone brushes
the bruise on my thigh. What is lust
doing here? Revelry? What is memory
doing here, pushing through the dizzying
crowd, its long boney hands that smell of the sea -
his smell - brine of boats. Boat bells chime.
Down the block at the street's low end the tide
pours in. Daylight's gone. Night stains the shore.

John Grey

Failed Attempt

I saw the garage door flung open
and the kid dragged out of the driver's seat
down the driveway, onto the grass.
Someone turned off the ignition.
Someone called the ambulance.
Someone shouted, "He's breathing!"
I saw death up close only it wasn't death.
It was wanting to die and why the ones
who drove him to it didn't want that to happen.
They stood around, mostly helpless,
but relieved, every one.
Only the fault breathed its last.
Died in that car when the ambulance got there.

Brigit Truex

On the Fifth Anniversary of Katrina
(August 5, 2010)

Not till the lavender hour
do you accept
the wail that snakes

from the burnished horn,
shimmering, daring you
to question its pain

seeping into your room
again, a blue tide
to submerge the bloom
of mold fledging the walls,

its corrosion creeping down
to meet the high-water mark
rippling the faded paper, roses
that somehow kept their heads

above it all, the solitary shoe,
the soggy wrapper, its red
plaid pattern optimistic
brilliant against

the brown surge sucking
all your hopes under.

henry 7. reneau, jr.

good times, my ass!!

let's rendition dreams and aspirations

or better yet, blindfold religious faith
and push it to the wall

cigarette hanging limp from its incredulous lips

          let's kick down optimism's door

        and drag it to a concentration camp
        let it make lemonade from lemons

            in Guantanamo Bay

let's tighten the noose

around Lady Liberty's charity and grace
and let that bitch swing in the breeze

        let's put the jackboot to blind hopes

           and wishes
       with their fairy-dust wide-eyed wonder

        and peter pan i-can-fly conviction

let's lubricate hate with some 30 weight

from Iraq and Kuwait
gag peace and duct-tape it to a chair

        then bring on the water-board
        and behavioral modification!

Lyn Lifshin

The mad girl feels she's had an affair with NASA

and now has
herpes, or is
knocked up
with something
worse, finds out
things almost
exploded before,
that he was more
concerned with
money.
She doesn't want
his double talk,
doesn't want a
cover or business
as usual. Some
thing in her dis-
solves as fast
as those 7 bodies,
a metal that lurched
then sank into
where it could tear
the bottom out if
you came too
close.

Anna Erickson

My Glass Jaw

The blow's thrown
Violent like exploding light bulbs.
My shoulder blades snake down the wall
And with heavy-lidded eyes
I fight darkness
And curse
My glass jaw.

On the hardwood
I stir beneath the foot on my chest
I gasp for breath, swallowing teeth like expired pills.
He picks off bits of my skin.
Sometimes I pick until I bleed.

I walk on eggshells
Till he wakes
Then I'm slipping on raw yolks
My friends tell me "those the brokes
And everything brakes at some point."

I push back
But my hands slip through like ghosts
My knuckles
Soft
I don't know why
I let him stay.
Not him.
He. She. Me.
This sexless, bodiless weight
That wears me down like tire tread.

Like the schizophrenic man on the corner
I punch
Kick
Slap
At the air
And find myself out of breath.
When we pass store windows
He has no reflection
And I turn my head slow
Like in water.

Arionó-jovan Labu'

Quitting Juanita

This time—

not goinna drown
my sorrows
gallons red
coconut rum,
entertain thoughts
swallowing a bottle
cyanide pills,
sniffing lines
of anthrax.

This time—

won't catch me
gasping for breath
listening sappy
bluez ballads.
Catching teardrops
in cupped palms
praying Jah
mend the broken
between us.

This time—

abstain
consoling grief
through ole' photos,
juxtaposed in
nostalgic details,
cuddled within
your ghost like
i'd developed
narcotic dependency.

This time--

be damned
entertain any
rebellious notions
forgiveness
act as if
some premeditated
accident
triggered by
fates of lust.

Oh no- no- no . . .

This time--

this time
be the last time
I luv you.

Geoff Stevens

Stay With Me Till Morning

Now that I've found you
the ideal word
the perfect line
do not disappear in my dreams
before I write you down
but stay with me
stay with me till morning.

Contributors

Heather Altfeld teaches composition in the English Department at California State University, Chico. In her free time, she likes to be silly with her children, cook, and walk the family cats and the golden retriever at night. As a practicing and publishing poet, she was recently invited to attend the Squaw Valley Community of Writers.

JoAnn M. Anglin of Sacramento is a member of Los Escritores del Nuevo Sol (Writers of the New Sun) and the Writers' Circle. Besides a chapbook, *Words Like Knives, Like Feathers* (Rattlesnake Press), her work is in *The Sacramento Anthology: One Hundred Poems*, the *Anthology of the Third Sunday Poets*, *The Pagan Muse*, and *Voces del Nuevo Sol*, as well as other regional publications.

Gaylord Brewer is the founding editor of *Poems & Plays*. His most recent books are the poetry collection *The Martini Diet* (Dream Horse) and the novella *Octavius the 1st* (Red Hen). He teaches at Middle Tennessee State University and in the low-residency MFA program at Murray State.

Alan Catlin has published dozens of chapbooks and full-length books of prose and poetry. His latest include "Near Death in the Afternoon on Becker Street" (March Street Press) and the forthcoming "Deep Water Horizon," ekphrastic oil spill poems (Pygmy Forest press). He was recently nominated for his twentieth Pushcart Prize.

Robert Childers, born in 1953, grew up 20 miles north of the Golden Gate Bridge. In 1974 he fulfilled his boyhood dream of moving to Alaska. He went to college, married, and raised a family. He earned degrees in Natural Resources, but then found his true passion – teaching second grade. After 20 short and happy years of teaching, he retired and now lives in the interior city of Fairbanks where he studies archaeology and poetry.

Philip Dacey is the author of 11 books of poems, the most recent being *Mosquito Operas: New and Selected Short Poems* (Rain Mountain Press, 2010). His previous was *Vertebrae Rosaries: 50 Sonnets* (Red Dragonfly Press, 2008).

David Dickson is an English Language Arts teacher for Northville Public Schools, in a small community west of Detroit, Michigan. He also coaches Cross

Country and Track. Married for 27 years, with three young adult children, Dave has recently published several poems in *The Rockford Review* and *Pegasus Review*.

Anna Erickson is a native of Sacramento. She presently lives and works in the heart of the city, capturing its people, places and energy in her poetry.

Briony Gylgayton has won multiple awards including a second for the 2010 Ina Coolbrith Memorial Poetry Prize and wins for both the poetry and fiction categories in the 2010 Pamela Maus Contest. Her manuscript of poetry about psychological disorders was awarded the Elliot Gilbert Memorial Prize in 2010. She is the publicist and co-producer for the Davis Poetry Night Reading Series.

John Grey, an Australian born poet, has been a US resident since the late seventies. He works as a financial systems analyst and has published in publications such as the *Connecticut Review, Alimentum*, and *Writer's Bloc* with newer work upcoming in *Pennsylvania English, Prism International*, and the *Great American Poetry Show*.

Brad Henderson (AKA, Beau Hamel) teaches engineering and scientific writing at UC Davis. His poetry has appeared in *Pedestal Magazine, Flatmancrooked's Slim Volume of Contemporary Poetics I, Squaw Valley Review, Poetry/LA*, and others. He is the author of two poetry chapbooks and the Phi Kappa Phi Award winning rock 'n' roll novel, *Drums*, recently re-released as a Kindle e-book.

Dennis Hock, a recently retired English professor, is the author of *The Secret Cup: Poems of Grief and Healing*. Instrumental in helping to develop Sacramento's Sutterwriters in 2003, he continues to work in hospitals and retreat centers with groups who use expressive writing as a healing process.

Arionó-jovan Labu' is an Afro-Cubano freelance writer, painter, and musician. His writing credits include the *African American Review, Drumvoices, Xavier Review, Obsidian, California Quarterly, SN&R*, and *Struggle*, to name a few. He is currently working on a documentary of his family's diaspora from West Africa to Cuba to America.

Lyn Lifshin has written 120 books and edited 4 anthologies. Her most recent book, *Ballroom*, is forthcoming. Her other recent books include *The Licorice Daughter: My Year With Ruffian* (Texas Review Press), *Another Woman Who*

Looks Like Me (Black Sparrow at Godine), following *Cold Comfort*, and *Before It's Light*. Website: **www.lynlifshin.com**.

Fred Longworth, a lifetime San Diego resident, restores vintage audio components for a living. His poems have appeared in numerous print journals, including *Caesura, California Quarterly, The Pacific Review, Pearl, Pudding Magazine, Rattapallax*, and *Spillway*. Online publications include *kaleidowhirl, Melic Review, miller's pond, Stirring*, and *Strong Verse*.

Joanne Lowery's poems have appeared in many literary magazines, including *Birmingham Poetry Review, Eclipse, roger, Cottonwood*, and *Poetry East*. Her most recent collection is the chapbook *Scything*, published (FutureCycle Press). She lives in Michigan.

Richard Luftig, a professor emeritus of educational psychology and special education at Miami University in Ohio, is a recipient of the Cincinnati Post-Corbett Foundation Award for Literature and a semi finalist for the Emily Dickinson Society Award. His poems have appeared in numerous journals in the United States (including *Art Times*) and internationally. Dos Madres Press published his third chapbook.

Clint Margrave has recent or forthcoming work in *The New York Quarterly, 3AM, Pearl, Chiron Review, Nerve Cowboy, The Teacher's Voice, Spillway*, as well as in the forthcoming anthologies *At the Gate: Arrivals and Departures* (Kings Estate Press) and *Beside The City of Angels: An Anthology of Long Beach Poetry* (World Parade Books). He lives in Long Beach, CA.

Gene McCormick's twelfth book, *Livin' The Blues At Cranky Jack's Bar & Grill*, a chapbook (MuscleHead Press/Boneworld Publishing), has just been released. Other poetry/fiction titles from McCormick include *Naked Skeletons* (2010); *Tanya, Queen Of The Greasy Spoon* (2009); and *Rain On The Sun* (2008). He lives in Wayne, Illinois, leading the good life of a writer and dog walker with his Australian Cattle Dog, Daisy.

Joyce Odam has published 100's of poems, including the *Christian Science Monitor, Rattle, Seattle Review, The Lyric*, and *Bellingham Review*. Her numerous awards include Grand Prize winner of the Artists Embassy International's Dancing Poetry Contest ('99). Among several reviews she has edited, currently she co-edits "Poet's Corner" for *Senior Magazine*. For more of her work, **www.rattlesnakepress.com/Joyce_Odam.htm**.

Frank Praeger is a retired biologist who lives in the Keweenaw, which is a peninsula that juts out of the Northwest portion of the Upper Peninsula of Michigan into Lake Superior. His poetry has been published in various journals in both the UK and the USA.

henry 7. reneau, jr. has published in many journals and anthologies, including *Tryst Magazine*, *Nameless Magazine*, *The Chaffey Review*, *Blue Moon Literary & Art Review*, *Pachuco Children Hurl Stones*, *BlazeVOX 2KX*, *FOLLY Magazine*, *The View From Here*, and more. He has also self-published a chapbook entitled *13hirteen Levels of Resistance*. His favorite things include Rottweilers, books of relevance to reality, and his "fixie" bike.

Marie Reynolds, a native of San Francisco, has lived most of her adult life in Sacramento. She is a registered nurse who works with children and their families. Her poems have appeared online and in print journals, including *Poetry Now*, *Rattlesnake Review*, and *Ekphrasis*.

Timothy Sandefur is an attorney and author in Sacramento, California.

Geoff Stevens is a British poet and editor of *Purple Patch* poetry magazine since 1976. His own poetry is published regularly around the world, and his current book is *Islands In The Blood* from the U.K. publisher *Indigo Dreams*. Website: **www.geoffstevens.co.uk**.

Brigit Truex has lived in the Sierra foothills for the past decade. Her work has appeared in reviews such as the *Atlanta Review*, *Canary*, *The Aurorean*, and *Manzanita*, as well as anthologies such as *I Was Indian*, *Vwa: Poems for Haiti*, and *The Sacramento Anthology: One Hundred Poems*. Her other collections include *Satuit Seasons*, *Leaf by Leaf*, and *Of A Feather*. *Rattlesnake Press* published the latest, *A Counterpane Without*.

Penelope Vaillancourt was born and raised in San Francisco, California, and has been influenced by various writers such as Jack Micheline, Charles Bukowski, Ntozake Shange, and others. She has published two poetry books, *Plutonium Poems* and *Tongues*. She currently resides in Northern California with her husband, two children, and granddaughter.

James Valvis lives in Issaquah, Washington. His poems or stories have appeared in many reviews and journals, including *5 AM*, *Atlanta Review*, *Confrontation*, *Nimrod*, *Potomac Review*, *Rattle*, *Southern Indiana Review*, and are forthcoming in *Arts & Letters*, *Crab Creek Review*, *New York Quarterly* and more. A collection of his poems is due from Aortic Books next year.

Marilyn Wallner returned to the classroom in her eighth decade, taking creative writing and poetry classes at American River College and the Sacramento Poetry Center. Vida, her toy poodle muse, accompanies Marilyn wherever she goes. She has been published in the *American River Review* and elsewhere, and although she has no computer, her daughter informed her that she has a "web presence."

Changming Yuan, twice nominated for the Pushcart prize, is the author of *Chansons of a Chinaman* (2009) and *Politics and Poetics* (2009). He grew up in a remote Chinese village and published several books before moving to Vancouver, where he teaches. His poems have been published in *Barrow Street*, *Best Canadian Poetry*, *Cortland Review*, *Exquisite Corpse*, *London Magazine* and more than 250 other literary publications worldwide.

About the Staff

Linda Collins, co-editor, lives and writes in Carmichael, CA. She studied English Lit at Vanderbilt University and has served on the board of the Sacramento Poetry Center for two years. Her poems have appeared in Sacramento area publications and on Garrison Keillor's *A Prairie Home Companion* website.

Theresa McCourt, co-editor, MA, received the 2008 Albert and Elaine Borchard Fellowship in poetry and also graduated from the Artist Residency Institute through the Sacramento Metropolitan Arts Commission. Her work has appeared in *The Squaw Valley Review*, Bill Gainer's *Magnet Project*, *Peter Parasol*, and elsewhere. For eight years, she also wrote bi-weekly columns for *The Sacramento Bee*.

Richard Hansen, cover designer, designs books of all sizes, but prefers them smaller than a business card. In 2001 he started Poems-For-All, a project to "scatter like seeds" tiny books of poetry.

Susan Davis Hyman, graphic designer, is a freelance writer and editor in West Sacramento. She writes fiction, nonfiction, and poetry. Her website: **www.commbysusan.com**.

Thomas Leaver, cover artist, is a painter and a teacher. He lives above a dojo in Oakland, CA. For more of Leaver's work, please visit McKenzie Fine Art Inc, New York, at **www.mckenziefineart.com**.

Notes

"Mockingbird," by Dennis Hock: previously published in *County Lines: The Poetry of Sacramento*, by Bob Stanley, Sacramento Poet Laureate, 2009-11, on the Sacramento Metropolitan Arts Commission at **www.sacmetroarts.org** and in the *Sacramento Press*, Sept 13, 2009 at **www.sacramentopress.com**.

"Poppies: Parallel Poem," by Changming Yuan: previously published at *Honey Land Review*, Fall 2010, Volume 3, Issue 1, at **www.thehoneylandreview.com**.

"The Horses at Night," by Lyn Lifshin: previously published in *Tattoo Highway (Issue TH/19—Reflections/Refractions: Bend, Break or Bounce)* at **www.tattoohighway.org**.

"Bar'd," by Clint Margrave: previously published in *Beggars and Cheeseburgers*, October, 2010 at **http://beggarsandcheeseburgers.wordpress.com/**

We Welcome Your Submissions
for the next *Tule Review*

Please read our current submission guidelines at

**http://sacpoetrycenter.wordpress.com/
category/tule-review/**

Email submissions to:
tulereview@sacramentopoetrycenter.org

Mail hard copy submissions to:
Sacramento Poetry Center
Tule Review
P.O. Box 160406
Sacramento, CA 95816